ELIZABETHAN ENGLAND

With thanks to Gary Sandling,
Ph.D. Candidate in the Department of History,
Yale University, New Haven, Connecticut,
for his expert reading of the manuscript.

CULTURES OF THE PAST

ELIZABETHAN ENGLAND

RUTH ASHBY

BENCHMARK BOOKS

MARSHALL CAVENDISH

NEW YORK

Benchmark Books
Marshall Cavendish Corporation
99 White Plains Road
Tarrytown, New York 10591-9001

Library of Congress Cataloging-in-Publication Data
Ashby, Ruth.
  Elizabethan England / by Ruth Ashby.
    p.   cm.— (Cultures of the past)
  Includes bibliographical references and index.
  Summary: Examines the history, culture, religion, and social conditions of
sixteenth-century England, during the reign of Queen Elizabeth I.
    ISBN 0-7614-0269-1 (lib. bdg.)
    1. Great Britain—History—Elizabeth, 1558–1603—Juvenile literature. 2.
England—Social life and customs—16th century—Juvenile literature. [1. Great
Britain—History—Elizabeth, 1558–1603. 2. England—Social life and customs—
16th century.] I. Title. II. Series.
  DA355.A3   1999
  942.05'5—dc20   96-43868

Printed in Hong Kong

Book design by Carol Matsuyama
Photo research by Debbie Needleman

Front cover: The Pelican Portrait of Queen Elizabeth I, by Nicholas Hilliard.

Back cover: A detail from Cornelius Visscher's 1616 view of London shows London
      Bridge spanning the Thames River.

Photo Credits
Front cover: courtesy of Walker Art Gallery, Liverpool/Bridgeman Art Library, London;
back cover: courtesy of The Granger Collection, New York; pages 6-7: Private Collection/
Bridgeman Art Library, London; page 8: Syon House, Middlesex/Bridgeman Art Library,
London; page 11: Private Collection/Bridgeman Art Library, London; page 12: Richard Philp,
London/Bridgeman Art Library, London; page 13: Houses of Parliament, Westminster,
London/Bridgeman Art Library, London; page 14: Bodleian Library, University of Oxford
(Poole Portrait number 38); page 15: Private Collection/Bridgeman Art Library, London; page
16: National Portrait Gallery, London/Bridgeman Art Library, London; pages 18, 24, 36, 45,
51, 55: The Granger Collection, New York; page 19: Woburn Abbey, Bedfordshire/Bridgeman
Art Library, London; page 21: National Portrait Gallery of Ireland, Dublin/Bridgeman Art
Library, London; page 25: British Museum, London/Bridgeman/Art Resource, NY; page 26:
Frick Collection, New York/Bridgeman Art Library, London; page 27: Musee de Blois,
France/Bridgeman Art Library, London; pages 28, 29, 38: Mary Evans Picture Library; pages
31, 33, 34: Stock Montage, Inc.; page 35: Louvre, Paris/Peter Willi/Bridgeman Art Library,
London; pages 37, 41: Victoria and Albert Museum, London/Art Resource, NY; page 40:
Belvoir Castle, Leicestershire/Bridgeman Art Library, London; pages 42-43, 57: Envision/VK
Guy, Ltd., Patrick Walmsley; page 44: Lambeth Palace Library, London/Bridgeman Art
Library, London; pages 49, 58, 60: Hulton Getty/Tony Stone Images; page 52: Musee Conde,
Chantilly, France/Giraudon/Art Resource, NY; page 54: Guildhall Library, Corporation of
London/Bridgeman Art Library, London; page 56: Private Collection/Bridgeman Art Library,
London; page 59: FORBES Magazine Collection, New York/Bridgeman Art Library, London;
page 64: Petrified Collection/The Image Bank; page 65: Private Collection/Bridgeman Art
Library, London; pages 66-67: Private Collection/Bridgeman Art Library, London; page 68:
Yale University Art Gallery, New Haven, CT/Bridgeman Art Library, London; page 69:
George E. Joseph; page 71: Walker Art Gallery, Liverpool/Bridgeman Art Library, London

CONTENTS

CHAPTER ONE

A PROUD LAND

This happy breed of men, this little world,
This precious stone set in the silver sea . . .
This blessed plot, this earth, this realm, this England . . .

Playwright William Shakespeare wrote these words praising his native land in 1595. It was a proud time for England. Queen Elizabeth had been on the throne and beloved by her subjects for thirty-seven years. The civil wars of the previous century seemed far away, and the land was united and at peace. Just seven years earlier, in 1588, England had defeated the Spanish Armada and established itself as a sea power. Already British ships were braving the rough waters of the Atlantic to explore the "new world" of the Americas. Most memorably, England was in the midst of a creative golden age. In the last fifteen years of Elizabeth's reign, poets, playwrights, painters, and musicians produced works of astonishing beauty and power.

Today what became known as the Elizabethan Age still conjures up an era of artistic brilliance and daring exploration. What were the circumstances that allowed such an era to flourish? To find out, we must go back to the chaotic years before Elizabeth's reign and explore England's past.

Invasion

The island of Britain lies to the west of the European continent, three hundred miles across the North Sea from Norway and twenty miles across the English Channel from France. To the west of Britain is the green and misty island of Ireland. At one time or another, the four lands that make up the British Isles—England, Scotland, Wales, and Ireland—have comprised from one to four nations. During the Elizabethan Age, England and Scotland were separate countries, ruled by their own kings and queens. Wales had been conquered by England in 1282 and was now formally united with its stronger neighbor. Ireland had been swept by rebellion after rebellion ever since Pope Adrian had granted Ireland to England in the twelfth century. The Irish resisted English rule and would continue to rebel throughout Elizabeth's reign.

Queen Elizabeth is carried in procession by her courtiers. The queen was revered by commoners and nobility alike.

William Shakespeare claimed that the "silver sea" surrounding Britain acted as a "wall" against invaders. In fact, intruders broke through the wall repeatedly. The original inhabitants of the isles are thought to have been a small, dark people. They were overrun by blond invaders from central Europe beginning in about 500 B.C.E.* The Celts, as the newcomers were called, were an imaginative people with a colorful mythology and an artistic culture. Their intricate stone crosses dot the landscape of Ireland to this day.

Britain was subsequently invaded by the Romans in 43 C.E.; Germanic tribes called the Angles, Saxons, and Jutes in the fifth century C.E; Danish Vikings in the ninth and early eleventh centuries; and French-speaking Normans in 1066. Each group came to plunder and exploit, and stayed to settle down and intermarry.

Richard III was king of England from 1483 to 1485. He was killed in battle with his successor, Henry VII.

Tudor England

During the Middle Ages (from about 476 to 1500), England was ruled by a series of kings from different royal houses. Sometimes the crown passed from father to son, but sometimes the royal line died out, and a distant relative succeeded to the throne. When kings were weak or the line of succession was uncertain, the nation was plunged into civil war. By 1485, a major civil war had been under way for thirty years. The country was wracked by a feud, called the Wars of the Roses, between two powerful families, the Lancasters and the Yorks.

In 1485, Henry Tudor, head of the House of Lancaster and the grandson of a widowed queen and her unmarried companion, defeated in battle the reigning monarch, Richard III, of the House of York. It is possible that Richard III was an unscrupulous man. He may have had his two nephews murdered in the Tower of London and his own brother executed in order to secure the throne. Nonetheless Richard was

*Many systems of dating have been used by different cultures throughout history. This series of books uses B.C.E. (Before Common Era) and C.E. (Common Era) instead of B.C. (Before Christ) and A.D. (Anno Domini) out of respect for the diversity of the world's peoples.

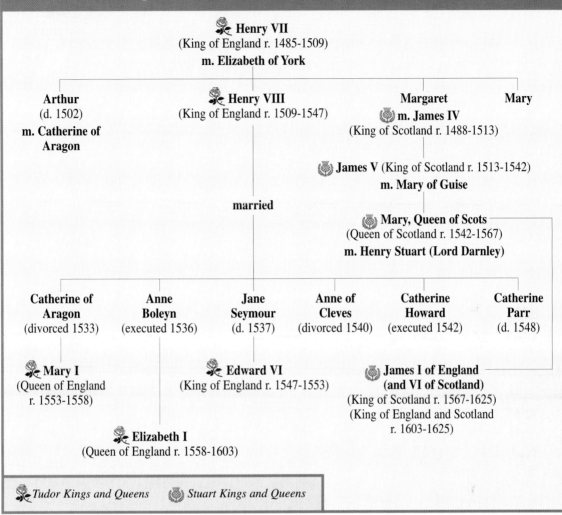

QUEEN ELIZABETH'S FAMILY TREE

Henry VII
(King of England r. 1485-1509)
m. Elizabeth of York

Arthur
(d. 1502)
m. Catherine of Aragon

Henry VIII
(King of England r. 1509-1547)

Margaret
m. James IV
(King of Scotland r. 1488-1513)

Mary

James V (King of Scotland r. 1513-1542)
m. Mary of Guise

married

Mary, Queen of Scots
(Queen of Scotland r. 1542-1567)
m. Henry Stuart (Lord Darnley)

| Catherine of Aragon (divorced 1533) | Anne Boleyn (executed 1536) | Jane Seymour (d. 1537) | Anne of Cleves (divorced 1540) | Catherine Howard (executed 1542) | Catherine Parr (d. 1548) |

Mary I
(Queen of England r. 1553-1558)

Edward VI
(King of England r. 1547-1553)

James I of England (and VI of Scotland)
(King of Scotland r. 1567-1625)
(King of England and Scotland r. 1603-1625)

Elizabeth I
(Queen of England r. 1558-1603)

Tudor Kings and Queens   *Stuart Kings and Queens*

the king, and by killing him and having himself crowned king, Henry Tudor ran the risk of being called a usurper. Throughout his subsequent reign, Henry took every opportunity to legitimize the House of Tudor.

Yet Henry VII, as he was now called, was a strong and determined ruler. He promptly disbanded the private armies that fueled the war and married a Yorkist, thus uniting the two families. The royal treasury had been emptied by countless wars, both at home and abroad. Henry VII established a new, more efficient system of taxation and refused to waste his money on war. He encouraged the wool trade with the European continent, commerce flourished, and England saw a new period of relative peace and prosperity.

When Henry VII died in 1509, he left the kingdom to his eighteen-year-old son, Henry. King Henry VIII was by all accounts a paragon of princes. Handsome, intelligent, and commanding, he was equally adept at languages, at hunting, and at dancing. Nothing but good fortune seemed to await the young king. Yet Henry VIII was also a man of huge appetites and little self-discipline. His zest for fighting led him into the incessant wars between France and Spain, and he lost much of the money his father had amassed. He also ate and drank too much. His large figure became corpulent, and by the end of his life the immense Henry VIII had to be lifted onto his horse by means of a block and tackle.

Henry's ego was just as large as his physique. Once he was king, Henry VIII insisted on doing precisely what he wanted. His domineering nature eventually brought him trouble. Henry's father had forced him to marry his brother Arthur's widow, Catherine of Aragon. (Henry was actually the second son of King Henry VII. Arthur had died when Henry was eleven.)

The most important role of a queen was, of course, to produce a male heir. Yet Catherine and Henry VIII had just one child who lived beyond infancy, a girl named Mary. By the time his wife was thirty-nine, Henry had begun to panic. At just this time he fell madly in love with one of the queen's ladies-in-waiting, Anne Boleyn.

In no time Henry was petitioning the pope at Rome for an annulment of his marriage. But an annulment would mean that the pope had to acknowledge that the marriage had never really been valid, and this he refused to do. At this juncture, Anne Boleyn became pregnant. Afraid that when the baby was born it wouldn't be legitimate, Henry persuaded the English clergy to declare his marriage to Catherine null. He married Anne, but when the baby was born it was a girl. Henry was bitterly disappointed and rapidly tired of Anne. After a few more years Anne had still failed to produce a male heir, so Henry had her falsely accused of infidelity. Anne Boleyn was beheaded in 1536, leaving behind her three-year-old daughter, Elizabeth.

His next marriage, to Jane Seymour, gave Henry a son, Edward, but Jane died in childbirth. Henry VIII was married three more times. The fate of Henry's six wives is neatly summarized: divorced, beheaded, died; divorced, beheaded, survived.

The most important consequence of Henry's marital woes was that

Henry VIII flirts with the vivacious Anne Boleyn. At right, Cardinal Wolsey, his foremost adviser, looks on with disapproval.

in order to get divorced, he had to break with the Roman Catholic Church. In 1534, Henry VIII issued the Act of Supremacy. It rejected papal control and declared the king (or queen) head of the English (later called the Anglican) Church. Thus England officially became a Protestant country.

During the reigns of the first two Tudor kings, three significant world events took place. First, the intellectual and cultural awakening in Italy, called the Renaissance, moved north. Second, in 1492, Christopher Columbus sailed west from Europe and laid claim to a new continent. Third, in 1517, Martin Luther started the Protestant Reformation. Together, these three events shook medieval Europe to its roots and ushered in a new age.

Edward VI, the young boy-king of England, died after a mere six years on the throne.

Henry VIII died in 1547 and was succeeded by his son, nine-year-old Edward VI. During Edward's reign, England became more securely Protestant. But he was a frail boy, and he died before his sixteenth birthday.

His half sister Mary, the daughter of the Spanish Catherine of Aragon, became queen at the age of thirty-seven. Devoutly Catholic, Mary I was determined to restore her country to the "true faith." She married a Catholic prince, Philip of Spain—later King Philip II—and prayed she would have children so that she could leave the throne to Catholic heirs. The English, always suspicious of foreigners, did not like this marriage at all. Then Mary lost the trust and affection of her subjects for good when she began persecuting Protestants. During Mary's reign, three hundred Protestants were martyred by being burned at the stake. Ever since, Mary Tudor has been known as "Bloody Mary."

Mary's short, unhappy reign ended when she died, childless, in 1558. She left England in the hands of her half sister, Elizabeth.

A New Queen for a New Era

After years of religious turmoil, England welcomed the new queen joyfully. Bells pealed the happy news, bonfires were lit across London, and people came out to feast and rejoice. Elizabeth's coronation on January 15, 1559, was a spectacular

Queen Mary I and Princess Elizabeth make a ceremonial entrance into London before Mary's coronation, August 3, 1553. England greeted its new ruler gladly, but Mary soon proved an unpopular queen. This nineteenth-century mural hangs in the House of Lords, Westminster, London.

show. But everyone asked the question: How will Elizabeth deal with the matter of England's religion?

Elizabeth I was Protestant like her mother, Anne Boleyn. By nature she was moderate in her religious opinions. Her greatest wish was for a strong and independent England, not one weakened by religious disputes. Immediately she reestablished Anglicanism throughout the country and made it the official religion. Elizabeth discouraged Catholicism, but for at least the first part of her reign Catholics were tolerated, as long as they didn't practice their religion openly or try to make trouble. Elizabeth discouraged fanaticism of all kinds.

She inherited a country deep in debt and weary of war. For centuries, Spain and France had fought to control Europe. Half Spanish herself, Queen Mary had pitted England on the side of Spain in this endless conflict. But her sister, Elizabeth, was frugal and peace-loving, like her grandfather Henry VII. She was determined to strengthen the economy at home and keep out of wars abroad.

As a first step, Elizabeth chose prudent men to be her councillors. Her chief adviser was William Cecil, who served her faithfully for forty years. It is said that when he was dying in 1598, his queen went to his bedside and fed him with a spoon. His son Sir Robert Cecil succeeded to his father's post.

William Cecil, Lord Burghley, was Elizabeth I's chief minister for forty years.

One of Cecil's foremost concerns was that Elizabeth marry. It was unusual for a woman to govern at all, much less alone, and besides, Elizabeth needed an heir. But the queen was too strong a ruler to want to be "ruled" by another. For twenty years, prince after prince vied for her hand. All negotiations eventually failed. But the ever-wily Elizabeth was able to use the promise of marriage as a diplomatic tool to strengthen alliances. As the balance of power in Europe shifted, Elizabeth negotiated with the princes of Spain, Sweden, Germany, and France, using herself as the prize, to keep England at peace. In 1572, she used marriage negotiations with the French Duke d'Alençon to enlist French aid against Spain.

The English Parliament also wanted Elizabeth to marry. Parliament, a legislative body founded in the Middle Ages, consisted of the House of Lords and the House of Commons. Initially the House of Lords, composed of members of the nobility and bishops of the church, was more powerful. But by Elizabeth's day, the House of Commons had gathered strength. To a large extent, it was drawn from a cross section of English society: townsmen and countrymen, the sons of nobles, merchants, and craftsmen.

In Elizabethan England, even though the queen was the undisputed ruler, Parliament represented the people. Queen Elizabeth

QUEEN ELIZABETH I (1533-1603)

Elizabeth Tudor was only three years old when her mother Anne Boleyn was beheaded. She spent her childhood in a series of castles under the watchful eyes of guardians and tutors. Unlike most women of the day, Elizabeth received a fine classical education; she proved to be intelligent and gifted at languages. Her tutor Roger Ascham offered nothing but praise: "Her mind has no womanly weakness, her perseverance is equal to that of a man, and her memory long keeps what it quickly picks up." Throughout her reign, Elizabeth would astonish foreign emissaries by speaking to them in their own languages and then switching to Latin at will.

Brought up a Protestant, Elizabeth found herself in trouble when her half sister, Mary, came to the throne. To allay Mary's suspicions, Elizabeth was forced to renounce her Protestantism and, at least occasionally, attend Catholic mass. She didn't really fool anyone, but neither could she be accused of disloyalty to the crown.

Elizabeth was popular with the people of England even before she became queen. Afterward, she did her best to keep in touch with them. Every summer, she and her court set off on a royal progress through the countryside, staying in towns or at the estates of the wealthy. People flocked to see her; they came up to her open carriage to offer her flowers or ask for advice.

Elizabeth became identified in the public mind with England. By 1570, she was so well liked that she was known as the Virgin Queen or Good Queen Bess. Her court was a place of unparalleled splendor, of festivities and ceremonies. Every year, the court celebrated the anniversary of her coronation. Knights jousted in tournaments, and all London feasted and danced. Elizabeth herself loved plays, pageants, and especially dancing.

Elizabeth dances energetically with Robert Dudley, the earl of Leicester. The queen loved the courtly pursuits of music and dancing.

Elizabeth was very conscious of the image she presented to the people, and she was proud of her accomplishments. "I thank God," she once told her Parliament, "I am endowed with such qualities that if I were turned out of the realm in my petticoat, I were able to live in any place in Christendom." By all accounts, her intelligence and wit were remarkable. She bewitched her friends, charmed her enemies, and inspired her nation. Elizabeth did fall in love at least once, with Robert Dudley, the earl of Leicester. But it would have been an unsuitable match, and she knew she couldn't marry him. Instead, she cultivated a series of favorites—young men to whom she was particularly attentive—throughout her life.

As she grew older, the vain queen hid her wrinkles behind thick white makeup. She died in her bed on March 24, 1603, in her seventieth year. Just before she died, Elizabeth had her coronation ring sawed off her finger. Her long marriage to England was over.

Elizabeth I in her splendid coronation robes, c. 1559.

was careful to get Parliament's approval on all important matters. She also needed its consent to raise taxes whenever she required money to defend the country. Throughout her reign, Elizabeth was in conflict with Parliament on many issues, including her marriage, reform of the church, and free speech. One persistent cause of disagreement was Elizabeth's cousin, Mary, Queen of Scots.

Mary, Queen of Scots

Mary, Queen of Scots inherited the Scottish throne in 1542. She was also the great-grandaughter of King Henry VII and heir to the English throne if Elizabeth had no children. As a staunch Catholic in an age of religious turmoil, Mary could count on the support of many Catholics in England and on the continent. She even enjoyed the backing of the pope himself, a man of great political power.

Beautiful and headstrong, Mary could also be foolish—as when she married a foppish young man named Henry Stuart, Lord Darnley, in 1565. Darnley became jealous of one of her favorites, a musician named David Rizzio, and had him stabbed to death in Mary's presence. The unpopular Darnley was in turn murdered by a group of Scottish nobles led by the earl of Bothwell. In another fit of bad judgment, Mary married Bothwell. Finding herself blamed for Darnley's murder, Mary fled Scotland in 1568. She left behind a baby boy, James Stuart, who was Darnley's son.

Elizabeth offered Mary sanctuary in England. But the exiled queen was a dangerous visitor. For nineteen years, Elizabeth kept her in a series of tightly guarded castles. There Mary conspired against Elizabeth with various English Catholics and with the Spanish. After a number of warnings, Elizabeth was ultimately unable to ignore evidence of a plot against her. Parliament had always distrusted Mary and now insisted that the queen get rid of her troublesome cousin once and for all. Reluctantly, Elizabeth had Mary, Queen of Scots beheaded on February 8, 1587.

The Spanish Armada

Mary's death brought matters between Spain and England to a crisis. Before Queen Elizabeth came to the throne, Spain and England had been allies for eighty years. It was a valuable alliance, for Spain was the most

Elizabeth knights Sir Francis Drake on the deck of his ship the Golden Hind, *April 4, 1581. (Engraving, nineteenth century.)*

powerful nation on earth, ruler of most of the Americas. In 1493, after Christopher Columbus's first voyage, Pope Alexander VI had divided the lands of the New World, Africa, and Asia between Spain and Portugal.

Naturally, Elizabeth wanted to secure some of the wealth of these lands for England. With her approval, English ships began to trade in territories officially designated as Portuguese or Spanish. Bold sailors like Francis Drake and Walter Raleigh raided Spanish ships carrying gold and silver from New Spain to Europe. The queen herself owned shares in these ventures, and soon the royal coffers were filled with gold. In 1580, Drake sailed around the world in his ship the *Golden Hind*. He returned loaded down with Spanish treasure. The queen made 160,000 pounds (a huge sum in those days) from the trip and knighted Drake on the spot. Elizabeth was especially pleased that England was developing a navy of English galleons at no cost to the throne.

Spain regarded the English as no better than pirates. Even worse, in Spanish eyes, was their stubborn Protestantism, for when Mary, Queen of Scots was executed, the Catholic cause in

England was doomed. King Philip II of Spain decided it was time to save England for Catholicism and avenge the loss of Spanish treasure. He made preparations to invade England. He assembled a huge fleet of ships, called the Armada, to attack the English coast.

In July 1588, when the Armada sailed up the English Channel, the English fleet was ready. One night while the Spanish galleons were anchored off the coast of Calais in France, English commanders sent fireships—old hulks with flares and gunpowder—among them to spread confusion. When the English attacked the next morning, the Spanish command panicked. In

The Armada portrait of Elizabeth shows the triumphant monarch with her hand on the globe, standing between two paintings. On the left is the victorious English fleet; at right is the defeated Armada.

hasty retreat they decided to sail north, where the "invincible" Spanish Armada was wrecked by storms on the rocky shores of Scotland.

News traveled slowly in the sixteenth century. When Queen Elizabeth visited the military camp at Tilbury two weeks later, news of England's deliverance had not yet reached her. Perched on a great gray horse and wearing a silver breastplate, the queen rode among the soldiers. "Her presence and her words," wrote an eyewitness, "fortified the captains and soldiers beyond all belief." On August 9, 1588, she made a stirring speech to the troops:

> *I am come amongst you . . . being resolved, in the midst and heat of the battle, to live or die amongst you all; to lay down for God, my kingdom, and for my people, my honor and my blood, even in the dust. I know I have but the body of a weak and feeble woman; but I have the heart and stomach of a king, and a king of England too.*

Fortunately, the English soldiers never had to fight the Spaniards. When they learned the fate of the Spanish ships, the English people believed that they had been delivered by God. The defeat of the Armada was a turning point for England. Not only did England, and much of northern Europe, remain Protestant, but England began its emergence as a formidable sea power. By 1700, it had the greatest navy in the world, and it ruled the sea for the next two hundred years.

Explorations

At the time of Elizabeth's reign, Spain and Portugal led Europe in world trade and colonization. The English sailors and explorers of the 1570s and 1580s were boldly determined to catch up. Sir Humphrey Gilbert claimed Newfoundland for England in the late 1570s. In 1584, Sir Walter Raleigh organized the first voyage to North America, with orders from the queen to find a suitable location for a colony. The first colony, established the following year, ended in failure when the settlers severely antagonized the Native Americans. Raleigh named the land they had tried to settle "Virginia," in honor of Elizabeth, who was often called the Virgin Queen.

SIR WALTER RALEIGH   (1552-1618)

Soldier, courtier, explorer, politician, and writer, Sir Walter Raleigh exemplified the restless spirit of the Elizabethan Age. Born into an established, genteel family, he spent his youth fighting wars in France and Ireland. He arrived at Elizabeth's court at age twenty-seven and immediately caught the fancy of the queen. Legend tells us that he gained her favor by spreading his elegant cloak over a puddle so she could walk across it without muddying her shoes.

"Tall, handsome, and bold," as a contemporary described him, Raleigh was the most brilliant of the queen's favorites. Like Elizabeth, he loved to write poetry. He dedicated much of it to her, whom he called "Cynthia, the Lady of the Sea." Elizabeth rewarded his wit and attention by giving Raleigh large estates, royal offices, and a knighthood. He abruptly fell out of favor in 1592 when the queen found out about his secret marriage to one of her own maids of honor.

But Raleigh had other plans to pursue. One of his dreams was to gain a foothold for England in the Americas: "To seek new worlds for gold, for praise, for glory." Between 1584 and 1589 he outfitted five expeditions to Virginia, but the queen wouldn't let him go in person. None of the colonies was successful, but Raleigh had staked out a claim for England in North America.

Raleigh also decided to explore on the Orinoco River in South America and find the legendary city of gold, El Dorado. This time, he made the trip with his explorers. Of course, he never found the imaginary city. But his raids against the Spanish restored him to the queen's favor in 1597.

Unfortunately, his enemies convinced Elizabeth's successor, King James I (Scotland's James VI), that Raleigh had conspired to overthrow him. Raleigh spent fifteen years imprisoned in the Tower of London. He was released in 1617 in order to lead another expedition to find the gold of El Dorado. The expedition was a disaster. Raleigh came home, only to be beheaded shortly thereafter for political reasons. He left us his own philosophic epitaph:

Even such is time, which takes in trust
Our youth, our joys, and all we have,
And pays us but with age and dust,
Who in the dark and silent grave
When we have wandered all our ways
Shuts up the story of our days,
And from which earth, and grave, and dust
The Lord shall raise me up, I trust.

Adventurous Sir Walter Raleigh, a favorite of the queen, founded the colony of Virginia in 1585.

Undaunted, Raleigh raised more money and tried again. In July of 1587, eighty-nine men, seventeen women, and eleven children arrived on Roanoke Island off the shores of present-day North Carolina. Within a month, the settlers sent Governor John White back to England for badly needed supplies. Because of the war with the Spanish Armada, White was not able to return to the colony until August of 1590. He was met by silence. The houses were gone, the settlers had disappeared, and only the letters *CRO* carved into a tree hinted that the colonists might have fled to nearby Croatan Island. White never found them. To this day, the fate of the "lost colony" of Roanoke remains a mystery.

Despite the failure of Raleigh's expeditions, England was now eager to expand overseas. Within twenty years, Raleigh's Virginia Company would try again. In the meantime, news of exotic lands stirred the popular imagination. Two important agricultural products were introduced to Europe: the potato and the tobacco plant. Soon, smoking tobacco leaves in the manner of the North Americans became the new fad at court.

Elizabeth's Final Years

In 1588, the year of the Armada, Elizabeth was fifty-five years old. She lived for another fifteen years, the hardest period of her reign. Although she was still revered, her popularity suffered when the country went through a series of bad harvests in the 1590s. She also had trouble raising money, as the cost of government kept increasing. Her conflicts with Parliament remained. Puritan members continually urged her to reform the Anglican Church, which she refused to do. As the queen grew older, some of her subjects even started looking forward to her successor.

But the person who gave the queen the most trouble was her favorite courtier, Robert, the earl of Essex. Thirty-three years younger than the queen, Essex was handsome, gallant, and ambitious. Elizabeth would have been content to keep him by her side at court. But Essex longed for adventure, and he repeatedly became involved in wars and expeditions that cost the queen a great deal of money. After he begged her to do so, she sent him to Ireland to put down a rebellion. But Essex failed miserably and returned to England in disgrace. Now desperate, he tried to raise a rebellion in London, where he was very popular. His plot was discovered, his supporters disappeared, and the earl of Essex was beheaded on February 25, 1601.

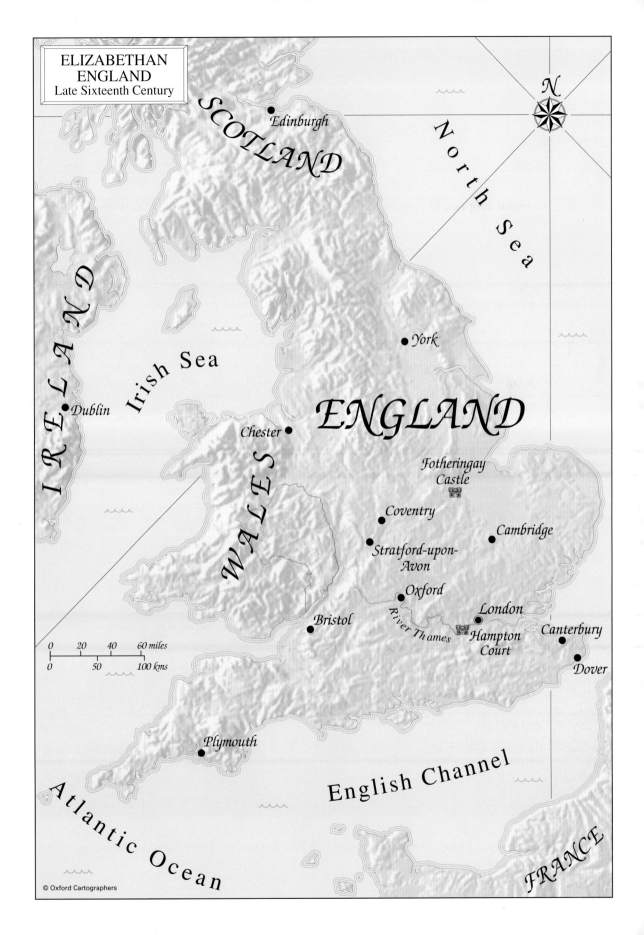

ELIZABETHAN
ENGLAND
Late Sixteenth Century

SCOTLAND

North Sea

Edinburgh

IRELAND

Irish Sea

Dublin

York

ENGLAND

Chester

Fotheringay
Castle

WALES

Coventry

Cambridge

Stratford-upon-
Avon

Oxford

Bristol

River Thames

London

Hampton
Court

Canterbury

Dover

0   20   40   60 miles
0   50   100 kms

Plymouth

English Channel

Atlantic Ocean

FRANCE

© Oxford Cartographers

Elizabeth presides over the opening of Parliament, 1586. Members of the House of Lords are seated on the floor of the chamber, bishops to the left, nobility to the right. Members of the House of Commons stand in the foreground.

Tired and discouraged, Elizabeth knew her reign was coming to an end. In November she met with her last Parliament and gave what became known as her "Golden Speech." For the last time, she referred to the strong bond between herself and her country: "It is not my desire to live or reign longer than my life and reign shall be for your good. And though you have had, and may have, many mightier and wiser princes sitting in this seat, yet you never had, nor shall have any that will love you better."

A year and a half later, the queen became sick. Her last act was to name James VI of Scotland, the son of Mary, Queen of Scots, successor to the crown of England. On March 24, 1603, the queen died. England was so stable that succession was peaceful and smooth.

Queen Elizabeth had always put her country first. Her critics might call her vain, changeable, and stingy. But she was also forward-thinking, responsible, and wise in ruling her country. When most of Europe was embroiled in religious and territorial wars, Elizabeth kept her country united and relatively at peace. During her forty-four-year reign, England became a first-rate power with a great navy. Commerce and industry prospered, and overseas colonization began. Elizabeth also presided over one of the greatest flowerings of the arts the world has ever known. After her death, the people of England looked back to the extraordinary era during which she had reigned and gave it her name: the Elizabethan Age.

Four black horses pull Elizabeth's funeral chariot. On top of the coffin rests a wooden effigy of the queen.

CHAPTER TWO

A GOLDEN AGE

The peace and prosperity of the Elizabethan Age gave people the opportunity to turn their attention toward the arts. Since it was an era of scholarship and exploration, artists were constantly challenged by new ideas and discoveries about the world. The music, art, and especially the literature they produced marks the Elizabethan Age as one of the most creative periods in human history.

The Renaissance

The golden age of English culture would not have been possible without the Renaissance in Europe. The Renaissance (the word means "rebirth") started in Italy in the fourteenth century and spread across Europe, reaching England during the reign of King Henry VIII. It brought a new emphasis on classical scholarship, called humanism, and on the individual person.

Humanism was the study of classical Latin and Greek literature and philosophy. Humanists approached life with a new spirit—one of inquiry and questioning rather than acceptance of "authorities," which had characterized European thought during the centuries under the rule of the Church. Scholars and poets such as the Italians Petrarch (1304–1374) and Dante (1265–1321) read the classics in the original Latin or Greek and based their own writings on classical models. Although the classics were known in the centuries preceding the Renaissance, humanist scholars boasted that between antiquity and their own day there had existed only a "dark middle age." This is how the ten centuries between the fall of Rome and the Renaissance came to be known as the Middle Ages.

Humanist studies celebrated the dignity of man, encouraging

Sir Thomas More helped bring the new learning of the Italian Renaissance to England. This painting is by Henry VIII's court painter Hans Holbein the Younger.

This French painting from 1591 shows Sir Thomas More being arrested by Henry VIII's soldiers. More was sent to the Tower of London, tried, and beheaded for refusing to acknowledge Henry VIII as head of the Church of England.

a life of virtuous action. The ideal Renaissance man was an all-around athlete, artist, poet, soldier, and courtier. Henry VIII was called the "perfect Renaissance prince" when he was young. In Queen Elizabeth's court, the poet and soldier Sir Philip Sidney and the explorer Sir Walter Raleigh earned their reputations as Renaissance men.

English and Italian scholars brought humanism to England in the early sixteenth century. Sir Thomas More (1478–1535) was one of the best known of the early humanists. He was Henry VIII's tutor when the prince was young and established a school of philosophy in his own home. His book *Utopia* (1516) criticized contemporary society by creating an image of a perfect country. Henry respected More and made him his Lord Chancellor. But when More refused to recognize the king as head of the English Church, Henry had his old tutor executed.

Johannes Gutenberg is believed to have been the first European to print with movable type.

One of the most important innovations of the Renaissance was the invention of the printing press. During the Middle Ages, books had to be painstakingly written out by hand. Printing with movable type was invented by Johannes Gutenberg in Germany in the 1450s and brought to England by William Caxton in 1476. Printing made books much more available to scholars and eventually to common people.

Poetry

By the time Queen Elizabeth came to the throne, classical and European models of poetry were well known among the upper classes in England. Suddenly poetry was all the rage at court. Nearly everyone—soldiers, courtiers, lawyers, and explorers—tried his or her hand at writing verse. Queen Elizabeth herself often expressed her private emotions in poetry. Not surprisingly, it was often good.

Elizabethan poetry was elegant and flowery, and usually about love. It was governed by certain set rules, called conventions. One of the most popular poetic conventions was the pastoral. Pastoral poems idealized life in the countryside, making it seem simpler and more innocent than city and court life. One of the most famous Elizabethan poems, "The Passionate Shepherd to His Love," by Christopher Marlowe, describes this ideal world, inhabited by shepherds and shepherdesses:

> *Come live with me and be my love,*
> *And we will all the pleasures prove*
> *That valleys, groves, hills, and fields,*
> *Woods, or steepy mountain yields.*
>
> *And we will sit upon the rocks,*
> *Seeing the shepherds feed their flocks,*
> *By shallow rivers to whose falls*
> *Melodious birds sing madrigals.*

Another poetic convention was the sonnet and the sonnet sequence. A sonnet is a fourteen-line poem with a set rhythm and rhyme pattern. In the Renaissance, sonnets owed their popularity to a series of sonnets (called a "sequence") written by the Italian poet Petrarch. Addressed to a woman named Laura, the Petrarchan sonnets express the many moods of being in love: joy, despair, tenderness, melancholy, and self-consciousness. Petrarch's poetry was so influential in Europe that poets imitated him for centuries. The most famous Elizabethan examples are Sir Philip Sidney's *Astrophel and Stella,* a sonnet sequence (published in 1591), and all of William Shakespeare's sonnets (published in 1609).

The sixteenth century's longest and most ambitious English poem was *The Faerie Queene* (1590–1596), by Edmund Spenser. This epic attempts to construct the ideal knight by following the adventures of twelve separate heroes, each representing a moral virtue, such as holiness or courtesy. (Spenser was able to complete only six books of the twelve he planned.) The individual

William Shakespeare reads to Queen Elizabeth. Although we do not know whether or not such a scene ever took place, we know that Elizabeth was a great patron of poetry and the theater.

SHALL I COMPARE THEE TO A SUMMER'S DAY?

Shakespeare's sonnets explore the many moods of love. But they also deal with time, beauty, and poetry. In Sonnet Number Eighteen, Shakespeare begins with a question and then answers it:

> Shall I compare thee to a summer's day?
> Thou art more lovely and more temperate.
> Rough winds do shake the darling buds of May,
> And summer's lease hath all too short a date.
> Sometime too hot the eye of heaven shines,
> And often is his gold complexion dimmed,
> And every fair from fair sometime declines,
> By chance or nature's changing course untrimmed;
> But thy eternal summer shall not fade
> Nor lose possession of that fair thou ow'st,
> Nor shall death brag thou wander'st in his shade
> When in eternal lines to time thou grow'st.
> So long as men can breathe or eyes can see,
> So long lives this, and this gives life to thee.

The young person for whom the poem was written is lovelier and more permanent than a summer's day, the speaker says. A summer's day can be too hot or too cloudy, and summer will always turn to fall. But the subject's eternal summer (youthful beauty) will not fade or die as long as the poem itself lives. This sonnet, the poet claims, will grant immortality.

knights are in the service of the Faerie Queene, who represents Elizabeth herself. *The Faerie Queene* is no dry moralistic poem. It is set in a magical realm of castles, dragons, witches, enchanted maidens, and evil monsters. Above all, the Elizabethans liked their literature to be entertaining.

Theater

The greatest triumph of the English Renaissance was the English theater. Before the 1550s, English drama was restricted to plays on religious themes, usually performed on religious holidays. In the beginning of

Elizabeth's reign, English drama came into its own for two reasons: the influence of the Renaissance and the establishment of theaters in London.

The Renaissance brought classical models to England, and classical Roman plays gave the English drama a whole new range of subjects. Roman comedies can be summed up by the familiar formula: boy meets girl, boy loses girl, boy gets girl. Roman tragedies trace the rise and fall of great men. They are violent and bloody and full of supernatural powers like

English theater began long before the Renaissance. It started inside the churches as small plays meant to illustrate the services. Gradually, the plays moved outdoors to church squares and village courtyards and drew hundreds of visitors. In the illustration above, amateur players in the town of Chester perform a "mystery play"—one that depicts stories from the Bible—on a movable stage.

ghosts. Elizabethan dramatists freely borrowed from these plots and added some of their own.

Before 1576, English actors belonged to traveling troupes. They performed on makeshift (although these could be quite elaborate) stages in village courtyards, castle halls, or the yards of inns. In 1576 an actor named James Burbage built the first theater in London, calling it simply The Theater. It was followed by the Curtain, the Rose, the Swan, the Globe, and the Fortune.

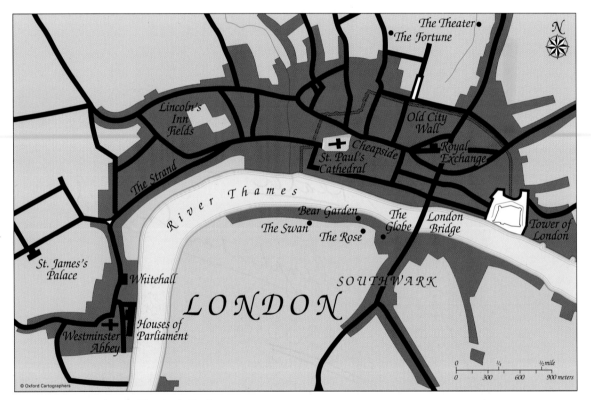

London in Elizabeth I's day

City authorities disapproved of theaters; theaters attracted crowds of ne'er-do-wells. So dramatic companies were forced to build theaters on the outskirts of London, next to other disreputable places like cockpits, bear gardens, and taverns. No Elizabethan theaters are left standing today. But from archaeological discoveries, we know they were polygonal in shape, with three tiers of galleries surrounding a yard with an open roof. They generally held about 2,000 to 3,000 spectators. In the yard or "pit" stood the "groundlings," who paid just a penny for the performance. Well-to-do merchants and the nobility sat in the galleries, where seats cost more.

The stage itself projected into the pit and was no more than forty feet across. It had two doors for exits and entrances, a trapdoor in the floor leading to "hell" (when the play called for such a place), and a balcony above signifying heaven. Props were few and suggestive. One tree would stand for a whole forest. A battle might consist of four or five actors, a few wooden swords, and bladders of sheep's blood. Scene changes relied on written signs and the imagination of the audience: "the Roman forum,"

This view of the inside of the Swan Theater shows the layout of the typical Elizabethan theater.

Audiences were lively in Shakespeare's day. Here, a performance of Shakespeare's Henry IV *takes place at the Globe, amid shouting and smoking and gossiping. (Painting, late nineteenth century.)*

"a wood outside Athens." Because all plays were performed during the daytime, night might be indicated by someone walking across the stage with a flaming torch.

Yet on these bare stages and before these mixed audiences, many of the greatest plays of all time were performed. Today the plays of Thomas Kyd, Christopher Marlowe, Robert Greene, and Ben Jonson are still read and still performed. But the greatest of all Elizabethan playwrights, and the greatest genius of English literature, was William Shakespeare.

The Drama of Shakespeare

William Shakespeare's professional career spanned only about twenty-three years. Yet in this time he wrote at least 37 plays, 2 long narrative poems, and 154 sonnets. His output alone is impressive. But it is the quality of Shakespeare's work that astounded his contemporaries and amazes us.

Shakespeare's plays are often divided into three periods. From 1589–1600, he wrote mainly historical dramas about England, which he alternated with comedies and one tragedy, *Romeo and Juliet* (1594). Then came tragicomedies like *Measure for Measure* and a series of magnificent tragedies, beginning with *Hamlet* (1600). His final period (1608–1613) consisted mostly of romances, plays of fantasy and wish-fulfillment.

Shakespeare's greatness stems primarily from two qualities of his writing: the psychological acuteness of his character portrayals and the brilliant inventiveness of his language. He has given us some of the most memorable characters in literature: Hamlet, the melancholy prince of Denmark; Falstaff, the braggart soldier; Iago, the master deceiver; Lady Macbeth, the ambitious queen. Characters come to life through brilliant dialogue and dramatic monologues called soliloquies.

Hamlet, *one of Shakespeare's greatest tragedies, has been performed constantly ever since its first production in 1601. This is an interpretation of the play's famous graveyard scene by the French painter Eugène Delacroix, 1839.*

William Shakespeare, the greatest dramatist in English history. This portait was done by an unknown artist in 1609.

William Shakespeare is probably the most famous writer who ever lived. It was his good fortune to have been born in a time that was extraordinarily favorable for literature and to have been able to make the best of his opportunities.

Though people have been fascinated by Shakespeare for four centuries, we actually know little about him. We don't know his exact date of birth, but we do know that William Shakespeare was baptized on April 26, 1564, in a small town named Stratford, about four days' trip by foot from London. The son of a middle-class glove maker, young Will would have gone to the local schools to learn how to read and write and, later, to study Latin and Greek. Unlike other famous writers of the day, Shakespeare never went on to study at either of the universities, Oxford or Cambridge.

Instead, he married Anne Hathaway, the daughter of a local farmer, in 1582. She was twenty-five, eight years older than he. They immediately had a little girl, followed by twins. Now the young man had a family to support.

What convinced Shakespeare to go into the theater? It's interesting to speculate. He must always have known he was a good writer. And he must have seen traveling troupes of actors as they passed through Stratford. At some time between 1585 and 1592, Shakespeare joined one of these companies as a minor actor and playwright.

All roads led to London in Elizabethan times, and London was where Shakespeare went. Within four or five years, he had established himself as the most promising young playwright in the country. By 1594 he had joined the Lord Chamberlain's Men and he never changed companies again. (The Lord Chamberlain's Men changed its name to the King's Men when King James I came to the throne.) The major actors of the company were shareholders who earned profits from the performances. With his share of the money, Shakespeare was able to buy land and a farm in Stratford. By the time he retired in 1613, Shakespeare was a wealthy man.

Shakespeare himself never published his plays, nor were they published during his lifetime. They belonged to the company, and if they had been printed, other troupes might have performed them. Shakespeare died on April 23, 1616. Not until 1623 did two of his fellow actors publish the First Folio, the first printed collection of Shakespeare's plays.

Shakespeare's contemporaries recognized his genius. After his death, fellow playwright Ben Jonson wrote a memorial poem, in which he stated that Shakespeare was "not for an age, but for all time." His words have proved prophetic.

Surprisingly, Shakespeare rarely invented his own plots. He adapted stories from history, old legends, and classical drama, and often made major changes to suit the story to the stage. His plays are full of the elements that Elizabethan audiences liked best: love, war, murder, treason, fairies, ghosts and witches, lovely maidens, dashing heroes, crude clowns and wise fools, perfect good and blackest evil. A few representative plots give some idea of Shakespeare's diversity—and why his contemporaries flocked to see performances of his plays.

Twelfth Night (1599)

Shipwrecked in a strange country, a young girl named Viola decides to disguise herself as a boy. She enters the service of Orsino, duke of Illyria, who woos the maiden Olivia. Olivia rejects the duke but immediately develops a crush on Viola, thinking she is a young man. Viola, for her part, falls madly in love with Orsino. Then Sebastian, Viola's twin brother, comes ashore and falls for Olivia, who thinks he is Viola. Olivia loves Viola, who loves the duke, who loves Olivia—who, as it turns out, really loves Sebastian. At the end, everyone finds his or her rightful match. Like most of Shakespeare's comedies, *Twelfth Night* is a comedy of mistaken identities and true love rewarded.

Macbeth (1606)

Macbeth, a nobleman of Scotland, meets three witches on a heath. They prophesy that he will be king and that his friend Banquo's children will be kings. Macbeth immediately begins to fantasize about seizing the crown. Egged on by his ambitious wife, Macbeth murders the king while the ruler is a guest at Macbeth's castle. Macbeth does become king, but he is haunted by guilt. Distrustful of Banquo, he has him murdered but then sees Banquo's ghost at a banquet. The other nobles recognize Macbeth's guilt and turn against him, Lady Macbeth commits suicide, and Macbeth goes down in bloody defeat.

A 1911 poster for Macbeth *pictures Macbeth's encounter with the three witches.*

38

The Tempest **(1611)**

Prospero, the duke of Milan, and his daughter, Miranda, have been marooned on an island by his brother and the king of Naples. There Prospero has become a magician and learned to control the elements. He has two servants, Ariel, a spirit of nature, and Caliban, a witch's child. Using his powers, Prospero shipwrecks his brother, the king, and the king's son, Ferdinand, on the island. With the help of Ariel and Caliban, Prospero makes his enemies repent their deeds. Miranda and Ferdinand fall in love, and Prospero regains his dukedom. *The Tempest* is full of magic and enchantment, with the kind of happily-ever-after ending that only fantasy can bring.

Shakespeare was aware that his plays were not real life. But he also knew, as one of his characters in *As You Like It* says, how closely reality could resemble a play:

> *All the world's a stage,*
> *And all the men and women merely players:*
> *They have their exits and their entrances;*
> *And one man in his time plays many parts.*

Art and Architecture

When England became officially Protestant in 1534, the country was cut off from the art of the Italian Renaissance, the art of Raphael and Michelangelo. Artists were discouraged from traveling to Roman Catholic Italy, and any painting that looked Italian was suspect. Instead, England turned to Protestant northern Europe for inspiration. Henry VIII brought painter Hans Holbein the Younger from Switzerland, and he became the official court painter.

Holbein is known for his realistic paintings of Sir Thomas More, Henry VIII, and other members of the court. Carefully rendered, his life-like portraits capture the essence of the subject's personality. After four

Caliban is portrayed as a brute savage and Ariel as an airy sprite in this 1911 illustration of a scene from The Tempest.

Hans Holbein's portrait of Henry VIII displays in lush detail the power and grandeur of the Renaissance monarch.

hundred years, Henry VIII appears as massive and domineering to us as he must have seemed to the English of his day.

Under the reign of Elizabeth, most notable court painters continued to be foreigners, usually Dutch. Some people have said that the English genius is for literature and not for painting. Certainly the English Renaissance did not produce art that was as great as its drama or poetry. But one native English painter did stand out among the rest: Nicholas Hilliard.

A favorite of Queen Elizabeth, Hilliard was a miniaturist. That is, he painted tiny paintings on lockets and other jewelry. His portraits were decorated with delicate flowers and plants, for Elizabethans liked their art to be ornamental.

Elizabethan architecture was also ornamental, though on a much grander scale. The second half of the sixteenth century was a great era of domestic building. As money came into the country from foreign trade, the wealthy built great palaces. Fortified castles were replaced by country houses, and medieval moats and drawbridges were transformed into pleasure gardens. Often built in the shape of an E (for Elizabeth), the new homes were covered with decorative details: huge leaded windows, domes, and gables. The wealthy usually built in stone or brick, but the middle classes constructed their half-timbered houses with huge wooden beams and plaster.

Elizabethans loved flowers, and they spent as much time planning their gardens as they did building their homes. Gardens were laid out like a series of outdoor rooms. There would be a kitchen garden, with herbs and vegetables, a garden of fruit trees, and a flower garden laid out in a mazelike pattern. Gardeners chose flowers for their color and symbolic

Nicholas Hilliard's Young Man Leaning Against a Tree Among Roses *reveals the Elizabethan love of decorative art. This miniature painting is only 2 3/4" wide by 5 3/8" deep.*

41

value: roses and daisies for purity, violets for faithfulness. Topiary, bushes clipped into realistic shapes, became popular. A contemporary described the fantastic topiary at Elizabeth's Hampton Court in 1599: "They were all manner of shapes, men and women, half men and half horse, sirens, serving maids with baskets, French lilies . . . all true to life."

Music

A visitor once described the England of Elizabeth as a "nest of singing birds." Music was everywhere: in the home, at court, on the stage, at church. Wandering minstrels stood in the center of town on market day, singing ballads and selling ballad sheets with pictures. The literate and illiterate alike could memorize tunes about love, heroes, and epic duels.

All educated people were expected to be able to sing complicated songs by reading music at sight. Soloists would accompany themselves on instruments such as the lute, an instrument plucked like a guitar, or the virginal, a small harpsichord. Much music, like the popular Italian madrigal, was written for multiple voices. Each singer would sing an individual melody and harmonize with the others.

English composers like William Byrd, Thomas Tallis, and Thomas Morley wrote both sacred and secular music. All short or "lyric" poetry was meant to be sung, as anyone who has ever been to a Shakespearean play knows. The music was sweet and sad, like the old song "Willow, Willow" in *Othello*; or it was light and carefree, like "There Was a Lover and His Lass" in *As You Like It*. Everyone agrees that during the Renaissance, English music reached its height.

Half-timbered cottages like this one still dot the English countryside.

CHAPTER THREE

DIVINE ORDER

Toward the beginning of the sixteenth century, a religious movement began that transformed Christian Europe. It was called the Protestant Reformation. People questioned their deepest beliefs and the customs of their ancestors. The controversy the Reformation touched off caused great turmoil. The disturbance was not as destructive in England, however, as it was on the European continent. This was due to the nature of the English Church and the British belief in order and hierarchy.

Christianity and the Reformation

When Queen Elizabeth came to the throne, Christianity had been the established religion in western Europe for more than ten centuries. Christians believe that a Jewish prophet named Jesus is the Son of God and the second person of the Trinity, the three-part Godhead. Faith in Jesus Christ earns the believer salvation and everlasting life. After Jesus' death, around the year 30, disciples and missionaries preached the gospel, or "good news," throughout the Mediterranean world. The Roman emperor Constantine made his empire Christian after he converted to Christianity in 312. Gradually all the pagan lands of the north were converted.

Almost from the beginning, a hierarchy of priests and bishops ran the Church and ministered to the faithful. The bishop of Rome, called the pope, was the supreme head of the Church. By the Middle Ages, the Roman Catholic Church was the most powerful institution in western Europe. (Eastern Europe had its own Eastern Orthodox Church.)

With power often came corruption. Church favors were bought and sold, and sometimes priests cared more for wealth

Religion played a vital role in the daily lives of Queen Elizabeth and her subjects. This frontispiece to the queen's prayer book shows Elizabeth at prayer.

Martin Luther fastens his Ninety-five Theses to the church door in Wittenberg, October 31, 1517. (Engraving, nineteenth century.)

than for religion. To many people, the sale of indulgences seemed especially outrageous. People could buy indulgences in order to receive an official church pardon for their sins. In 1517, a German priest named Martin Luther wrote down his objections (called "theses") to indulgences on a large manuscript. On October 31, he nailed his document to the cathedral door in Wittenberg, Germany. His act of defiance started the Protestant Reformation.

Protestants (protesters) wanted to reform the Christian Church by ridding it of corruption and returning to the Bible as the guide to life. By reading the Bible themselves, rather than relying on priests and bishops, they would become responsible for their own salvation. Many Protestant sects got rid of the hierarchy of the Roman Catholic Church and substituted ministers (instead of priests) to lead individual congregations. They also made the Bible available to ordinary people. In the Catholic Church, all services and the Bible were in Latin, which few people could understand. One of the first things Martin Luther did was translate the Bible into German.

Luther opened the door to dissent, and Protestantism spread like wildfire across Europe. It brought terrible religious wars in its wake. In 1580, an Englishman of Elizabeth's court reported that on the continent there were "depopulations and devastations of whole provinces and countries, overthrowing, spoiling and sacking of cities and towns, imprisoning, ransoming, and murdering of all kind of people." The situation was different, he said, in England, where "the peaceable government of her Majesty doth make us to enjoy all that is ours in more freedom than any nation under the sun at this day."

How did Elizabeth keep this fragile peace?

The English Compromise

As we have seen, England did not completely escape religious tumult. Queen Mary's reign had its share of martyrs. But Elizabeth made haste to restore the Anglicanism of her father. The Church of England represented a compromise between Catholicism and Protestantism. Like Catholicism, it was run by a hierarchy of clergymen and bishops. But Elizabeth herself, not a foreign pope, was at its head. Anglican services, like those of other Protestant denominations, were in the country's native tongue, not in Latin. But England had its own liturgy, the Book of Common Prayer.

Most important, Elizabeth made religion almost identical with nationalism. She was not terribly concerned about what people really believed, so long as they practiced their non-Anglican faith in the privacy of their homes. But Elizabeth did insist that in public, religious order be maintained. Strict laws required every grown person in the nation to attend the Anglican Church every Sunday and holy day, or pay a fine. England quickly became a nation of steady churchgoers.

Together with the monarchy, the Church was the central institution of Elizabethan society. The most important moments in one's life were celebrated at the parish church, in the rituals of baptism, marriage, and burial. The church was where people first heard important news from the wider world, where they gathered with family and friends to worship and to celebrate, and where they learned as children, in Sunday-afternoon catechisms, the elements of their faith and the importance of duty and obedience.

At first, Catholics were tolerated if they practiced their faith discreetly. Tragically for many English Catholics, in 1570 Pope Pius V excommunicated Elizabeth and officially "deposed" her from the throne. Many Catholics were torn between allegiance to their church and loyalty to their country. Those who didn't declare their first allegiance to Elizabeth could be declared traitors and put to death. The papal excommunication, together with the Spanish Armada and the conspiracies of those who wanted to put Mary, Queen of Scots on the English throne, intensified anti-Catholic feeling throughout Elizabeth's reign.

Protestants who wanted to separate from the Anglican Church were also persecuted. They could be deported, imprisoned, or even executed for practicing or preaching their religion. There were some Catholic and Protestant martyrs in Elizabeth's day, too.

The Idea of Order

Elizabethans believed above all in the concept of order. Everything in the universe had a place and a purpose. God ruled over the universe, the king ruled over the kingdom, and the husband ruled over the wife. God had decreed the role each being was to play in creation. As a contemporary writer stated:

> *Every kind of trees, herbs, birds, beasts, and fishes have a peculiar disposition [given] unto them by God their creator; so that in every thing is order, and without order may be nothing stable or permanent.*

Elizabethans visualized order as a "Great Chain of Being," with each link in the chain as a part of God's creation. The chain stretched from

HOLIDAYS

Elizabethans worked hard and played hard. When England was a Roman Catholic country, there were more than one hundred holy days a year. By Elizabeth's time, that number was down to only twenty-seven. But Elizabethans still observed these holy days (the origin of our word "holiday"), as well as many other traditional celebrations.

Each season of the year had its special occasions. On May Day (May 1), everyone went "a-maying" to celebrate the coming of summer. A contemporary wrote: "See the young men and maids, old men and wives run gadding overnight to the woods, groves, hills and mountains, where they spend all night in pleasant pastimes." The next morning the merrymakers planted the flower-covered maypole and danced around it, each holding on to a gaily colored string.

In August, the country folk celebrated the gathering of the harvest with feasts and dancing. November in London brought the Lord Mayor's Show. Crowds gathered on the riverbank to watch boats decorated with characters from Greek mythology or English legend parade up and down the Thames River. Afterward, a procession of floats wound through the London streets featuring, for example, Neptune on a lion, Father Thames on a sea horse, Robin Hood and his Merry Men.

The grandest festivities of the year were held at Christmas. For twelve days, from December 25 to January 5 (Twelfth Night), work stopped throughout the country. In households great and small, hospitality and entertainment held sway. Guests feasted on capons and hens, turkeys, geese, ducks, beef, and mutton. Music played and young people danced, while the elderly sat in comfort by the fire.

At court, the Master of Revels planned entertainments that lasted every night until early in the morning. Players like Shakespeare's Lord Chamberlain's Men performed their plays. (They presented *Twelfth Night* to the queen in 1601.) The most spectacular of entertainments was the masque—a mixture of dance, song, disguise, and spectacle.

The year ended with New Year's Day, when everyone gave and received presents. One year the earl of Leicester gave the queen "a very fair jewel of gold, being a clock fully furnished with small diamonds and rubies." Like her subjects, Elizabeth loved holidays.

May Day was a time of revelry in town and village alike. In this nineteenth-century engraving, the artist imagines what May Day would have been like in an Elizabethan village.

God's throne down to inanimate objects. At the bottom were the elements, liquids, and metals. Then came the plants, then the lower animals, such as shellfish and worms, and the middle-level animals such as insects and fish. Next came the higher animals: the birds and the mammals. Above the animals were human beings, and above them were the angels, which were pure spirit, just as inanimate objects were pure physical matter.

Every class of beings and every being within that class could be ranked according to abilities. Fire was the first and most important among elements, the dolphin highest among fishes, the eagle greatest among birds, the lion superior among beasts, the emperor foremost among people.

Human beings held a middle position between animal and angel, earth and heaven. In a famous speech from Shakespeare's play, Hamlet praises people but makes it clear that though they may be like angels or gods, they are also like animals:

> *What a piece of work is a man! How noble in reason! how*
> *infinite in faculty! in form, in moving, how express and*
> *admirable! in action how like an angel! in apprehension, how*
> *like a god! the beauty of the world, the paragon of animals.*

Each individual had duties to uphold according to his or her place in society. When servants obeyed their masters and subjects obeyed their king, all was well. If not, chaos followed. Elizabethans knew only too well the suffering that could follow rebellion and treason.

In Shakespeare's plays, natural catastrophes often foreshadow human disasters. For instance, during the night when Macbeth kills Duncan, the earth shakes, the moon eclipses the sun, and horses break out of their stalls and eat each other. Authority and obedience were the bedrock not just of society but of the natural world.

Astrology

To Elizabethans, nature was a unified whole. They believed that the movements of the planets and the position of the stars affected human beings intimately. Astrology was a serious matter in the sixteenth century, partly because modern astronomy had not yet been widely accepted. In 1543, Polish astronomer Nicolaus Copernicus published the theory of modern astronomy. The earth, he said, revolves about the sun. Although some educated Elizabethans knew about Copernicus's theories, the Elizabethan view of the universe was still based on the theories of the ancient astronomer Ptolemy. He held that the earth was the center of the universe and that the sun and planets revolved around it. Above the planets were the heavenly spheres, to which the stars were fixed.

According to the theory of astrology, the heavens are divided into twelve segments, each named for a constellation and represented by a sign. Elizabethans believed that each of the twelve constellations of the zodiac had a direct effect on the human body. For instance, the sign of Leo ruled the back and heart, Taurus ruled the neck, and Cancer ruled the chest, stomach, and lungs.

An illuminated manuscript (c. 1472) portrays the four humors in action. Clockwise from top right: A melancholy man sings a sad song; a sanguine (optimistic) man woos a lover; a choleric man beats a woman; a phlegmatic man takes to his bed.

THE FOUR HUMORS

When you say you're in good humor, what do you mean? Probably that you feel happy about something. The word *humor* meant something very different to Elizabethans. They believed that all physical and mental health was governed by four humors, or fluids: black bile, phlegm, blood, and choler. Too much black bile could make one melancholy. An excess of phlegm, believed to come from the kidneys or lungs, made one slow and lazy. Optimistic or passionate people were said to be sanguine and were ruled by the blood, which was thought to come from the liver. Choleric or angry people were ruled by the spleen.

Medicine in the sixteenth century was still in a very primitive state, and physicians blamed all sorts of illnesses on an imbalance of the humors. Only if all four humors were in their correct proportion in the body would a person really be able to say that he or she was in "good humor"!

During the Renaissance, astrology was taught at universities as a science, and astrologers were much sought-after at court. Queen Elizabeth had her own personal astrologer, and she asked his opinion before beginning any major venture. Astrologers across Europe were alarmed at the movements of the stars and planets in 1588. Elizabeth was warned it would be a year of disaster. Instead, 1588 turned out to be the year of the Armada, of victory and celebration.

The twelve signs of the zodiac are shown exerting an influence on different parts of the human body in this fifteenth-century illustration.

CHAPTER FOUR

SOCIAL ORDER

Elizabethan society reflected a belief in a divinely ordained natural order. Authority and obedience were stressed from youth to old age, and at every stage of life an individual had a duty to perform.

Queen Elizabeth opens the Royal Exchange in 1570. The opening of the Exchange, the central meeting place for London's merchants and bankers, was a sign of the new business prosperity of the Elizabethan Age. This nineteenth-century mural hangs in the Exchange.

Distinct Classes

England lost more than a third of its population due to a horrible plague called the Black Death in the last half of the fourteenth century. It took a century to recover. By the sixteenth century, the population was rising rapidly. In 1603, the year of the queen's death, the number of people in England was more than four million.

Elizabethan England had distinct social classes. Above everyone was the royal family. Then came the nobility and the landed gentry, or gentlemen. (*Gentleman* is a traditional term for someone who does not engage in manual labor to earn a living.) Even though they comprised only 2 percent of the population, the nobles and the landed gentry (along with the church and the crown) owned most of the property in England. In order to keep family property intact, the law of primogeniture dictated that the eldest son of each family inherit the land and his father's title. This meant that the younger sons had to seek their own fortunes. They often went into the law, the church, or the military, and could become even richer or more renowned than their elder brothers.

Below the gentry was a group of people who might be considered a middle class: the clergy, prosperous businessmen, professional men, and yeomen (farmers who owned their own land). This middle portion of Elizabethan society, like the upper

A physician prepares medicinal oils in this woodcut from a medical textbook, 1576. Doctors, like lawyers, clergy, and businesspeople, occupied a middle rung on the Elizabethan social ladder.

one, could vote for members of Parliament and could hold important local offices.

Last came the craftspeople (like tailors, shoemakers, and carpenters), farmers, day laborers, and finally, the poor. As one writer said, the poor "have no voice or authority in our commonwealth." Even below them were the vagrants, those without any fixed abode.

Social differences were obvious. What were called sumptuary laws even decreed the kinds of clothes people in different classes might wear, though the rules weren't always enforced. The rich wore clothing made of fine wool and linen and silk, while the poor were dressed in leather and rags. The gentry ate wheat bread; the poor ate bread made of rye or barley. The rich

COURT COSTUMES

In portrait after portrait, Elizabethans come before us decked out in all their finery: silks and satins, brocades, velvets, jewels, and feathers. The clothing worn by the members of Elizabeth's court was unsurpassed in extravagance and richness. Made of the rarest and most costly materials, apparel was cut and molded, padded and rolled into fashionably outrageous shapes. The well-dressed courtier wore a padded vest called a doublet, silk stockings, and short, puffed breeches. To be fully dressed, he would need a cloak of finest velvet or satin, lined with silk and embroidered with gold, silver, or even pearls.

Women wore hooplike petticoats called farthingales. Placed over a thick roll at the waist, they could hold the skirt out at right angles a couple of feet. High, stiff ruffs held the neck upright. Worn by both men and women, ruffs could extend as much as nine inches from the neck. As a finishing touch, the wearer was draped and spangled with jewels—rubies and diamonds from Persia, emeralds from Colombia, topaz from Brazil. The whole world contributed to the adornment of wealthy Elizabethans.

Elizabeth's court was a place of high fashion and showy ostentation. This painting was done by Frank Moss Bennett, a twentieth-century artist.

lived in great houses of brick or stone; the poor in huts of sticks or dirt.

Yet despite strict social distinctions, there was actually a lot of movement between classes. Then, as now, the acquisition or loss of money could change a family's social status quite quickly. Let's say that in a year of bad harvests, a well-to-do yeoman farmer was able to buy up some of the land of his less-fortunate neighbors. He could send his son to one of the universities and then to the Inns of Court in London to become a lawyer. The son, now equipped with a gentleman's education, would be heir to a country estate worked by others. The sons of the neighbors, on the other hand, would be tenants on land their fathers had once owned.

Hard work and good luck could make a man a fortune in the sixteenth century. The many opportunities for increasing wealth and social advancement made Elizabethan England an energetic, enterprising society.

Women

Each household was a miniature of the wider world. The husband was the undisputed head, and under his dominance were his wife, children, and servants, if any. Law as well as custom established that wives were subordinate to their husbands. A writer giving advice to brides in 1617 wrote: "If ever thou purpose to be a good wife, and to live comfortably, set down this with thyself: mine husband is my superior, my better; he hath authority and rule over me; nature hath given it to him. . . . God hath given it to him."

Ideally, fathers in Elizabethan England arranged the marriages of their children in order to increase, or at least maintain, a family's wealth. It was a child's duty to submit to his or her parent's decision. In practice, of course, it didn't always work out

The Great Hall at Hatfield House recalls the splendor of the Elizabethan Age. Only the wealthiest nobles could build places such as this one, owned by Sir Robert Cecil and his family. A portrait of Elizabeth hangs on the wall to the right.

In this portrait of a prosperous Elizabethan family, the man who looks so confidently out at the viewer is clearly the head of the household. The wife, by contrast, regards only her husband.

this way. William Shakespeare probably married for love. Sir Walter Raleigh also married for love, and by doing so earned the queen's displeasure. Probably most Elizabethans married for love *and* money, and their parents sometimes had little say in their choice of mates.

Most women of the sixteenth and seventeenth centuries brought a dowry of cash or property to the marriage. The dowry went to the father of the groom. In return, the wife was guaranteed a "jointure," a chunk of property or money, if she was left widowed. Wealthy widows were very much in demand and might actually have the privilege of choosing their second husbands for themselves.

Generally speaking, when women entered into marriage, they lost all rights. Under law, husband and wife were one person—and that person was the husband. He controlled all his wife's personal property, such as clothes and jewels, as well as her land. He had the right to beat her when he chose and to oversee her religious life. He even governed her children.

Many couples actually enjoyed more equality in day-to-day living than the law dictated. They could truly be fond of each other and have a reasonable and practical relationship. In the working classes, a woman often contributed as much as her husband to her family's income. She could manage a shop, or raise the cows and chickens on a farm, or be in charge of spinning, weaving, or knitting in a cottage industry.

Children and Education

People in Elizabethan England lived, on average, only to the age of thirty-two. Life expectancy was so short in those days because of the appalling rate of child mortality. Between a quarter and a third of all English children died before they were fifteen. Most of these did not live to age one.

The older a child got, the more likely he or she would be to survive. Upper-class babies were sent away at birth to "wet nurses," who breast-fed them for the first year of life. They would

King Henry VIII plays with his son, Edward, while Princess Elizabeth looks on in this sentimental view of the royal nursery, painted in 1838. Like other upper-class children, Henry's offspring were raised by governesses and taught by tutors until they came of age.

return to their parents, only to be raised by a series of governesses and tutors. Boys would leave home again between the ages of seven and thirteen to go to boarding schools. Children of the working classes would also leave home, between the ages of ten and seventeen, to become servants, laborers, and apprentices in shops, farms, and the homes of the wealthy. It has been estimated that two of every three boys and three of every four girls lived away from their parents' home in adolescence.

By the time children were of marrying age—the average was twenty-seven for males and twenty-five for females—they had acquired the skills they would need to be fully functioning adults. Many had at least a rudimentary education. Most children

Students in Elizabethan grammar schools like this one spent eleven hours a day studying, with a break only for noonday dinner.

of the upper and middle classes (and some poor children as well) went to local elementary schools at about four or five. There they learned to read, write, and count. Girls went to these early schools too, although they never went on to the next stage, grammar school.

For older students, classes began early, at six o'clock in the morning, and ended eleven hours later, with only a brief recess. Shakespeare has left us a picture of "the whining schoolboy, with his satchel and shining morning face, creeping like a snail unwillingly to school." In grammar school, the emphasis was on Latin and Greek. Study was monotonous, dependent on memorization and rote learning. But the classics were necessary because in the sixteenth century all professionals—diplomats, lawyers, doctors, civil servants—conducted much of their business in Latin. It is interesting that not only children of the well-to-do but also many children of the poor were able to go to grammar school, the latter as scholarship students. The final stage, for one to be considered truly well educated, was to attend one of the two universities, Oxford or Cambridge.

At school, as in the rest of society, the emphasis was on duty and correct behavior. When the poet Sir Philip Sidney went away to grammar school in 1564, his father sent him a letter that summed up the way children were supposed to behave: "Be humble and obedient to your master, for unless you frame yourself to obey others, yea, and feel in yourself what obedience is, you shall never be able to teach others how to obey you."

Daily Life

It is always fascinating to imagine what daily life was like long ago. Luckily, in their literature and reminiscences, the Elizabethans have left us a picture of the way they lived.

In the country, the day began early, at three o'clock in the morning. The milkmaids got up to milk the cows and the farmer harnessed his oxen. The morning porridge was ready at four. In the city, folks might stay in bed a little later. But by six, schoolboys were off to school and shopkeepers had opened their shops, ready for the day's trade.

In the morning, everyone was at work. The merchant might see to his accounts, the shipbuilder would be on the docks. Even beggars took their customary positions on the highway or by a church door. Housewives were planning the day's meals, tending the sick, sewing, or

IF YOU LIVED IN ELIZABETHAN ENGLAND

If you had been born in 1585 during the reign of Queen Elizabeth I, your way of life would have been determined by the facts of your birth—whether you were a girl or a boy, wealthy or poor. With this chart you can trace the course your life might have taken if you were a member of a merchant's family.

You were born in London . . .

As a Boy . . .   As a Girl . . .

You live with your parents in a comfortable apartment above your father's shop on London Bridge. Your father is a merchant who sells silks, satins, other cloths, and small ornaments. From your bedroom you can hear the roaring of the Thames River beneath the bridge. Your parents are strict but loving, and you play a lot with your brothers and sisters.

At age 5 you attend a local elementary school, where you learn arithmetic and your ABCs. Every morning and evening you say prayers with your family.

▼

At age 8 you go to grammar school for eleven hours a day. There you study Latin and Greek grammar, logic, and rhetoric. You read and translate such Roman classics as Ovid's *Metamorphoses* and Virgil's *Aeneid.* For recreation, you may play chess, soccer, or hockey. You say your prayers and read your Bible daily.

▼

At age 13 you become an apprentice to a London merchant. When you're not working in the counting house, you slip out to see a play at the new Globe Theater, a tournament, or a pageant on the Thames.

▼

At age 27 you marry the daughter of a neighboring goldsmith. Soon you have your own business, selling tobacco from the new Virginia colony. You prosper and move into a fine house in the City of London. You are able to send your sons to Oxford University and to see your daughters well married.

At age 5 you attend an elementary school, where you learn to read, write, and count. At home, your mother teaches you to sew.

▼

At age 8 your schooling ends, but you continue to read the Bible daily. You work by helping with the accounts in your father's shop. Most of your time is spent learning to run a household. You help your mother supervise the servants, and you learn to cook, clean, sew, and embroider. You may take music or dancing lessons as well.

▼

At age 15 you leave home to become a maidservant for a noble London family. Your job is to wait upon the lady of the house. In your spare time, you have an active social life with the other young servants of the large household. You see your parents regularly, and you may go home to help out in times of need.

▼

At age 25 you marry a young shopkeeper you have known since childhood. With the help of your servants, you raise your children, run the household, and assist in your husband's shop. You are a hardworking and obedient wife, and you raise your children to be good Christians and loyal English men and women.

In old age, you are taken care of by your sons and daughters. When you die, you are buried in the family plot in the graveyard of the local Anglican church. You have been an observant Christian and die in the hope of resurrection with Jesus Christ.

embroidering. Girls not at school might take dancing lessons or practice their needlework.

The day's dinner would be at 11:00 a.m. All across the country, people dropped what they were doing to eat and socialize. For the plowman, dinner might be as simple as bread and cheese with a drink of cider. In a well-to-do home, dinner could be elaborate, with many dishes and courses: roast beef, veal, turkey, woodcocks and quails, salmon, sole, lobster and shrimps, peas, turnips and salad, fruit tarts, cheese, and of course, wine and beer. Understandably, the gentry might not rise from the table until 2:00 in the afternoon. The farmer, though, would take a nap after dinner and then resume his plowing.

In the afternoon, young men in town might attend a play or a bear-baiting. Merchants, shopkeepers, and housewives would go back to work. By the time the children were out of school at 5:00, it would be time for the evening meal, called supper. The day would be over for laborers, who needed to be up before dawn. But other folks might stay up for a while to play cards, sing songs, or tell stories. Then evening prayers, and "so to bed."

CHAPTER FIVE

A LASTING GIFT

The moment Queen Elizabeth died, her name and reign became legend. People looked back to the days of Good Queen Bess as a time of incomparable glory. The crowning event of her reign had been the defeat of the Armada. England had shown the world the strength of her navy and had emerged as a European power to be reckoned with. From then on, Spain slowly slipped into second-rate status, and England became a new leader in world trade and colonization. By the nineteenth century, the British Empire spanned the globe. Today, the cultural legacy of the Elizabethans lives on around the world.

The crown and scepter, symbols of British royalty.

England and the Americas

Sir Walter Raleigh never gave up on his dream to establish a British empire in the New World. "I shall yet live to see it an English Nation," he wrote to Sir Robert Cecil in 1602. He did not, but the voyages he organized paved the way for other Englishmen.

In 1607, just four years after the death of Elizabeth, three ships sailed up the James River in Virginia and established the first successful English colony. Captain John Smith kept Jamestown alive throughout the first harsh years by insisting that everyone pitch in and help out. "He that will not work neither shall he eat," he stated flatly. The colony found a way to make money by growing tobacco and exporting it to England.

More colonists soon followed. In 1620, religious separatists,

British ships bring provisions to settlers in Jamestown. Jamestown, founded in 1607, was the first permanent English settlement in the Americas.

called the Pilgrims, colonized the rocky northern land they named New England, and what is called the Great Migration was on. By 1640, more than 20,000 people had journeyed from England to Massachusetts.

English settlers brought English customs and habits with them. They brought their music, their games, their clothes, and their place names: New London, New York, New Bedford. They even brought their religion: Anglicans settled in the south, and Puritans, or Protestant separatists, settled in the north. For the first two hundred years, before the great wave of Irish and German migrations in the 1840s, North American immigrants were overwhelmingly English and Scottish in heritage. The first census of the new nation, taken in 1790, revealed that 64 percent of Americans traced their ancestry to the British Isles. (The second-largest group, at 18 percent, were African Americans, who had been brought forcibly on slave ships.)

The English settlers also brought their form of self-government. We have seen how the English Parliament in Elizabeth's day took the first steps toward popular representation. Elizabeth required the assent of Parliament—of "the people"—to make laws. In the colonies, far from London, colonists got into the habit of making laws for themselves. In Jamestown in 1619, settlers elected the first representatives to the Jamestown Assembly (later called the Virginia House of Burgesses). This was the first representative government in the English colonies. The forty-nine Pilgrim men who signed the Mayflower Compact in 1620 agreed to consult with one another to "enact, constitute, and frame, such just and equal laws . . . as shall be thought most [fitting] and convenient for the general Good of the Colony."

One hundred and fifty-six years later,

a young man named Thomas Jefferson stated unequivocally that any government derives its powers from the "consent of the governed." In other words, the people of a nation are its government. It may seem like a long way between the democratic ideals of the Declaration of Independence and the monarchical rule of Elizabeth. But the roots of American democracy lie in the Elizabethan cooperation between monarchy and Parliament, and in the English spirit of independence.

The Pilgrims land at Plymouth, Massachusetts, on December 11, 1620. This nineteenth-century print shows the bitter cold of the Pilgrims' first winter in North America (and dresses the Pilgrims in nineteenth-century clothes).

America's Founding Fathers sign the Declaration of Independence, July 4, 1776.

The English Language

English settlers also brought their language to the new land. Renaissance England's greatest gift to the world has probably been the English language. Of course the language existed before 1550, but it was spoken only by the inhabitants of a small island, and it was in the process of radical change. Just two hundred years before, the English had spoken the Middle English of Chaucer. Today, we find Chaucer's language barely recognizable. Yet we still read and understand the plays of Shakespeare, written four hundred years ago. Why is twentieth-century English so similar to late-sixteenth-century English? To find out, let's look at the state of the language in Shakespeare's day.

Because of the many invasions of the British Isles over the centuries, the English language as it had evolved by the sixteenth century had many sources: German, Latin, French, Old Norse, Celtic. The cultural vigor of the Renaissance added a profusion of

SHAKESPEARE'S LIVING LANGUAGE

The inventiveness of Shakespeare's language is probably unrivaled. London slang, court rhetoric, legal jargon, country proverbs—his plays have them all. In Shakespeare's works, the Renaissance love of words, and of extravagant words, finds its fullest expression. Shakespeare had a working vocabulary of thirty thousand words, compared to the fifteen thousand words of most well-educated people of today or the eight thousand of the King James Bible.

More than those of any other writer, Shakespeare's phrases have found their way into our everyday speech. To him we owe such familiar expressions as: "too much of a good thing," "the truth will out," "it's Greek to me," "my own flesh and blood," "without rhyme or reason," "at one fell swoop," "vanished into thin air," "as luck would have it," "to stand on ceremony," "I didn't sleep a wink," and many more, including "all's well that ends well." The next time you open your mouth to speak, you may be quoting Shakespeare!

James Earl Jones acts the part of Macbeth in a 1966 production. The plays of Shakespeare have been performed more times in more countries around the world than those of any other playwright.

new words, words like "education," "thermometer," "atmosphere," "skeleton," "gravity," "encyclopedia," "exaggerate," "contradictory." Words were coined so rapidly that there was a great debate about whether to accept all of them; many seemed faddish and unnecessary. But writers latched on to them and even invented their own. It is generally accepted that any word people find useful survives. It has been estimated that in the hundred-year period between 1520 and 1620, some ten to twelve thousand new words came into the English vocabulary.

Writers like William Shakespeare, Ben Jonson, Christopher Marlowe, and Francis Bacon reveled in the new expressiveness of their native language. They wrote in English, not Latin (as Sir Thomas More had in *Utopia,* written in just 1514). Elizabethan poems, plays, and essays were read in newly printed books by an increasingly literate populace. Then in 1611, a new translation of the Bible, authorized by King James I, was published. Written in beautiful, rhythmic prose, the King James Bible was the crowning glory of Renaissance English.

Two Books: Shakespeare and the Bible

For the next few centuries, all English-speaking Protestants—Anglican, Presbyterian, Congregationalist, Unitarian, and Baptist—read the Bible in the King James Version. (In the twentieth century we have a number of modern translations of the Bible, and the King James Version has slipped out of favor.) The King James Bible became the standard for spoken and written English. Immigrants setting off for a new land, pioneers crossing the plains of the American Midwest in a covered wagon, might have room to take just two books with them. Those two books were the Bible and the collected works of Shakespeare. Regional English accents might vary, but because everyone who could read English used the same books, there was a common language understood the world over.

In the eighteenth and nineteenth centuries, British shipping companies set up trading ports and then imperialist colonies around the world. Eventually English was spoken in places as diverse as Singapore, South Africa, and India. Though local languages survived, educated people in

Queen Elizabeth came to symbolize the brilliance of the age in which she lived. This is the Pelican Portrait by Nicholas Hilliard, so named for the pelican jewel on the queen's dress.

Africa and Asia often spoke English as the language of diplomacy or government. By the end of the twentieth century, the English language dominated the world. The international market for American television, movies, and music has established English as the first really global language, spoken by more people in more places than any language has ever been in the history of humankind.

Today, the English language has a vocabulary of more than five hundred thousand words (contrasted with French, for example, with fewer than one hundred thousand), and it continues to grow. In the spirit of Renaissance England, it expresses almost every new human discovery and experience with a new word. Yet it is still, recognizably, the language of Shakespeare.

In human history, only occasionally have the right people lived at just the right time to create a culture of lasting beauty and importance. The Elizabethan Age was one of these magical moments. We look back at it today with awe and longing. Yet we need only attend a performance of *Hamlet,* or *Twelfth Night,* or *The Tempest* to experience again, however briefly, the invigorating spirit of those far-off times.

Elizabethan England: A Chronology

1476   William Caxton prints first book in England

1485   Henry Tudor defeats Richard III at Bosworth Field and becomes Henry VII of England

1491   Henry VIII born

1492   Christopher Columbus makes his first voyage to the Americas

1509   Henry VII dies; Henry VIII succeeds

1517   Martin Luther starts the Protestant Reformation

1533   Elizabeth I born

1534   Henry VIII declares himself head of the Church of England

1536   Anne Boleyn executed

1547   Henry VIII dies; Edward VI succeeds

1553   Edward VI dies; Mary I succeeds

1558   Mary I dies; Elizabeth I succeeds

1564   William Shakespeare born

1584   Sir Walter Raleigh organizes first English expedition to Virginia

1587   Mary, Queen of Scots executed

1588   Spanish Armada defeated by England

1600   First performance of Shakespeare's *Hamlet*

1603   Queen Elizabeth I dies; James I succeeds

1607   Jamestown founded in North America

1611   King James Bible published

1616   William Shakespeare dies

1618   Sir Walter Raleigh executed

GLOSSARY

Anglican Church: the established Church of England, founded by King Henry VIII in 1534

astrology: the study of the influence of the stars and planets on human affairs

ballad: a narrative song, often with a stock refrain

bearbaiting: the setting of dogs upon a chained bear; bearbaiting was a popular form of entertainment in sixteenth-century England.

bear garden: an enclosed ring for bearbaiting

Book of Common Prayer: the service book used in the Church of England

classical literature: the literature of the ancient Greeks and Romans

cockpit: an enclosure for cockfights, bloody battles-to-the-death between roosters

comedy: a form of drama meant to amuse and with a happy ending

epic: a long, narrative poem with a serious theme and a central heroic figure

four humors: according to ancient medical theory, the four chief liquids of the human body: blood, phlegm, black bile, and choler

Great Chain of Being: medieval and Renaissance metaphor for the order of creation

half-timbered: constructed of wood timber with spaces filled with white plaster or brickwork

heath: a broad area of open, rolling infertile land with few plants except some shrubs; a wasteland

hierarchy: classification according to rank

indulgence: in the Roman Catholic Church, a pardon for punishment due for sin. The sale of indulgences was made unlawful in 1562.

madrigal: a Renaissance song, usually written for multiple voices singing in harmony

Middle Ages: the period in European history from the fall of the Roman Empire in about 476 to about 1500

Parliament: the legislative body of English government

pastoral: a poem that idealizes life in the countryside, making it seem simpler and more innocent than city and court life

primogeniture: in law, the exclusive right of inheritance by the eldest son

Puritanism: a reform movement within the Church of England that began during the reign of Queen Elizabeth I. Puritans wanted to "purify" the Church and do away with the hierarchy of bishops.

Reformation: the religious revolution within the Christian Church in Europe in the sixteenth century

Renaissance: the rebirth of classical learning that began in Italy in the fourteenth century and reached its height in Europe in the fifteenth, sixteenth, and early seventeenth centuries. It was marked by great accomplishments in literature, science, and the arts.

Roman Catholic Church: the Christian church headed by the pope, the bishop of Rome

separatists: in the sixteenth and seventeenth centuries, English Protestants who wanted to separate from the Church of England; Pilgrims, Anabaptists, and Quakers are some examples of separatist groups.

soliloquy: a dramatic monologue in which the speaker voices his or her thoughts aloud

sonnet: a fourteen-line poem with a definite rhyme scheme

topiary: trees and shrubs cut into decorative shapes

tragedy: a serious form of drama in which a heroic central character experiences a castastrophic reversal of fortune

FOR FURTHER READING

Brown. John Russell. *Shakespeare and His Theater.* New York: Lothrop, Lee and Shepard Books, 1982.

Bush, Catherine. *Elizabeth I.* New York: Chelsea House, 1985.

Frost, Abigail. *Elizabeth I.* Marshall Cavendish, 1989.

Garfield, Leon. *Shakespeare Stories.* New York: Schocken, 1985.

Haines, Charles. *William Shakespeare and His Plays.* New York: Franklin Watts, 1968.

Hodges, C. Walter. *Shakespeare's Theater.* New York: Coward, McCann and Geohegan, 1964.

Stanley, Diane, and Peter Vennema. *Bard of Avon: The Story of William Shakespeare.* New York: Morrow, 1992.

Stanley, Diane, and Peter Vennema. *Good Queen Bess: The Story of Elizabeth I of England.* New York: Four Winds Press, 1990.

Stewart, Philippa. *Shakespeare and His Theater.* London: Wayland Publishers, 1973.

White-Thompson, Stephen. *Elizabeth I & Tudor England.* New York: The Bookwright Press, 1985.

Zamoyska, Betka. *Queen Elizabeth I.* New York: McGraw Hill, 1981.

BIBLIOGRAPHY

Adams, Robert M. *The Land and Literature of England.* New York: Norton, 1983.

Briggs, Asa. *A Social History of England.* London: Weidenfeld and Nicolson, 1984.

Byrne, M. St. Clare. *Elizabethan Life in Town and Country.* New York: Barnes and Noble, 1961.

Holmes, Martin. *Elizabethan London.* New York: Praeger, 1969.

Laroque, François. *The Age of Shakespeare.* New York: Abrams, 1991.

Lees-Milne, James. *Tudor Renaissance.* London: B. T. Batsford, 1951.

McCrum, Robert, William Cran, and Robert MacNeil. *The Story of English.* New York: Penguin, 1986.

Neale, J. E. *Queen Elizabeth I.* Garden City: Doubleday, 1957.

Ross, Josephine. *The Tudors: England's Golden Age.* New York: G. P. Putnam's Sons, 1979.

Rowse, A. L. *The England of Elizabeth.* Madison: University of Wisconsin Press, 1978.

Smith, Lacey Baldwin. *The Elizabethan World.* Boston: Houghton Mifflin, 1991.

Still, Kathy. *The Elizabethan House and Garden.* San Francisco: Chronicle Books, 1987.

Stone, Lawrence. *The Family, Sex, and Marriage in England 1500–1800.* New York: Harper and Row, 1977.

Tillyard, E. M. W. *The Elizabethan World Picture.* New York: Random House, 1934.

INDEX

Page numbers for illustrations are in boldface

ABOUT THE AUTHOR

R uth Ashby has loved Shakespeare and Elizabethan England ever since she played a tree in a sixth-grade production of *Macbeth*. (Well, actually, it was a soldier disguised as a tree.) Hours of listening to Living Shakespeare records prepared her to study English literature at Yale University and for graduate work at the Universities of Michigan and Virginia, where she also taught some courses in Shakespeare's drama. Today she lives in her hometown of Huntington, New York, and works full-time as a children's book editor and CD-ROM producer. She looks forward to someday watching her daughter, Becky, in a school staging of *Macbeth*—maybe as Lady Macbeth, or better yet, one of the three witches!